5) Enforce sustainable conduct and workouts to keep a balanced domestic and thoughts for lengthy-term fulfilment.

6) Access real-lifestyles case research and examples demonstrating the effectiveness of Time wondering in numerous residing conditions.

7) Embrace a lifestyle of harmony, peace, and achievement by way of integrating Time questioning standards into your daily life.

Book 's Description:-

"Winning time & think manage: your house without Decluttering Your thoughts" is a transformative guide that explores the profound connection between domestic management and mental well-being. In this insightful ebook, readers will delve into the idea of Time questioning, an effective approach that allows individuals to effectively control their homes at the same time as assuaging issues, relieving anxiety, and putting off negative thinking styles.

through a series of realistic techniques and actionable advice, readers will discover ways to streamline their dwelling areas without overwhelming their minds. The ebook offers a complete knowledge of the way litter-loose environments contribute to mental clarity and emotional stability. via embracing Time wandering concepts, readers will discover how to prioritise responsibilities, prepare their houses, and create purposeful residing areas that foster peace and harmony.

Winning time & think manage: Your Home Without Declutter Your Mind.

INDEX

Chapter 1:   Page :- 14 to 19

Understanding the mind-domestic Connection :-

1) Exploring the hyperlink among intellectual litter and bodily muddle
2) Recognizing How your private home environment affects Your mental nicely-being

Chapter 2:   Page :- 20 to 30

The power of Time thinking :-

1) Introducing the idea of Time questioning
2) Understanding How Time thinking Can rework your private home and thoughts
3) Gaining knowledge of to Prioritise responsibilities and control Time effectively

Chapter 3:   Page :- 31 to 48

Overcoming worry and anxiety :-

1) Figuring out assets of fear and anxiety in your property and mind
2) Implementing strategies to manipulate and reduce tension stages
3) Cultivating Mindfulness Practices to stay gift and Calm

Chapter 4:

Page :- 49 to 59

Streamlining your private home surroundings:-

1) Simplifying Your residing area without Decluttering Your thoughts
2) Sensible suggestions for Organizing and keeping a clutter-free home
3) Growing functional and pressure-unfastened residing areas

Chapter 5:

Page :- 60 to 72

Casting off poor thinking styles:-

1) Recognizing and hard negative thoughts and ideals
2) Cultivating a nice attitude through Affirmations and Gratitude
3) Techniques for Overcoming Self-Doubt and Boosting Self-confidence

Chapter 6:

Page :- 73 to 80

Time thinking in movement: Case research and Examples:-

1) Real-lifestyles stories of people who've converted Their houses and Minds the use of Time thinking
2) Making use of Time questioning ideas to different residing conditions and challenges

Chapter 7: Page :- 81 to 93

Nurturing Sustainable conduct for lengthy-term fulfilment:-

1) Organising exercises and systems to preserve a Balanced domestic and thoughts
2) Integrating Time wondering Into Your everyday lifestyles for Lasting results
3) Hints for Overcoming Setbacks and Staying inspired

Chapter 8: Page :- 94 to 106

Embracing a existence of harmony and properly-being:-

1) Reflecting to your journey toward mental and domestic clarity
2) Celebrating Achievements and increase alongside the manner
3) Embracing a lifestyle of stability, Peace, and achievement

Bullet point: Page :- 4 to 5
Book Desription: Page :- 6 to 7
About the Author :- Page :- 8
Difference between time & mind management :- Page :- 9 to 13

Bullet point:-profit this book

1) Discover ways to manipulate your own home efficiently without feeling beaten by using muddle or intellectual pressure.

2) Discover sensible techniques to stop annoying and reduce anxiety stages related to domestic management.

3) Gain perception into the powerful concept of Time questioning and how it can rework each of your home surroundings and your mind-set.

4) Locate methods to cast off bad questioning styles and domesticate a tremendous mindset for stepped forward intellectual nicely-being.

"Time suppose" also offers valuable insights into dealing with anxiety and overcoming terrible idea styles that often accompany domestic control demanding situations. Readers will discover strategies for cultivating mindfulness, difficult self-doubt, and nurturing a high-quality attitude, in the long run leading to greater resilience and emotional proper-being.

Drawing from real-existence case studies and examples, the e-book illustrates the transformative impact of Time thinking across diverse residing conditions. Readers could be inspired with the aid of tales of individuals who've effectively incorporated Time thinking into their daily lives, experiencing profound changes in both their homes and their minds.

Whether or not you are struggling with clutter, anxiety, or negative questioning, "Time Suppose" provides the guidance and support needed to create a harmonious home surroundings and domesticate a peaceful attitude. With sensible tips, actionable strategies, and a compassionate approach, this ebook empowers readers to embody a lifestyle of balance, joy, and success.

Acknowledgments

Recognizing the Contributions and aid of these who've Helped alongside the manner.

About the Author :-

I am Elias Sterlingwood, Post Graduate. Solving the problem that my reader faces is my hobby and passion and I always keep in mind what my reader wants. I try to solve that problem as quickly as possible. I love writing this kind of content.

Time assumes: manipulate your property without Decluttering Your thoughts gives realistic steering and proposal for individuals in search of to create a harmonious living environment at the same time as nurturing their mental proper-being. Through the strength of Time wandering, readers will find out how to cultivate a clutter-lose domesticity and a peaceful mind, leading to a lifestyle of balance, pleasure, and achievement.

Elias Sterlingwood

Difference between time & mind management :-

Time management and mind management for the home are two distinct but interrelated ideas that make contributions to the overall efficiency, concord, and well-being of people and their living spaces. here are the important thing differences among time and mind management for the home:

Time management:

*Time control makes a speciality of the effective allocation and utilisation of time to perform tasks, chores, and obligations inside the home.
*It involves putting priorities, creating schedules, and organising sports to maximise productiveness and minimise procrastination.
*Time management strategies may encompass developing to-do lists, placing time limits, delegating tasks, and the use of productivity equipment together with calendars and apps.
*The intention of time management is to optimise the usage of time, lessen pressure, and growth efficiency in finishing household tasks and duties.

*Thoughts control relates to the law and management of one's mind, feelings, and intellectual state inside the domestic environment.

*It includes techniques for keeping a nice attitude, managing stress, and fostering emotional nicely-being amidst diverse challenges and duties.

*Mind management strategies might also encompass mindfulness practices, *Meditation, relaxation techniques, cognitive-behavioural techniques, and emotional regulation exercises.

*The intention of thought control is to domesticate resilience, internal peace, and mental clarity, thereby improving overall happiness and pride within the domestic.

Key variations:

*Time control mostly deals with the realistic aspects of organising and executing obligations within a targeted time-frame, at the same time as mind management specialises in the mental and emotional components of maintaining nicely-being and concord.
*Time management addresses external elements which includes closing dates, schedules, and priorities, whereas thoughts management addresses internal elements including thoughts, feelings, and attitudes.
*Time control is involved with performance and productivity in finishing family obligations, even as thought management is concerned with emotional resilience, strain reduction, and mental health.
*While time management enables individuals to accomplish greater things in less time, thought management allows individuals to maintain a nice outlook, address challenges, and experience a satisfying domestic lifestyle.

In summary, at the same time as each time control and mind control are essential for maintaining a properly-functioning home, they serve distinctive functions and require wonderful strategies for implementation. By integrating powerful time and mind control techniques, individuals can create a harmonious and effective domestic environment that nurtures both their sensible wishes and their emotional well-being.

Which management is better for success in our life:-

Determining which control approach is better for fulfilment in existence depends on character dreams, alternatives, and circumstances. Each time control and thought management play vital roles in reaching success, but they serve one of a kind purposes and are frequently intertwined. here is a breakdown:

Time control:

*Time control is essential for reaching productiveness, performance, and goal attainment.
*It facilitates individuals arrange their obligations, prioritise duties, and make the maximum in their to be had time.
*effective time management lets people fulfil deadlines, accomplish duties, and pursue their long-time period goals.
*It fosters discipline, consciousness, and accountability, that are critical characteristics for fulfilment in various components of existence, such as career, education, and personal development.

Mind control:

Mind control is vital for maintaining emotional well-being, resilience, and mental readability.

It includes regulating thoughts, emotions, and attitudes to reduce stress, decorate positivity, and domesticate internal peace.

Thought management techniques including mindfulness, meditation, and cognitive-behavioural strategies assist individuals address challenges, overcome obstacles, and thrive in adversity.

It fosters self-cognizance, emotional intelligence, and healthy coping mechanisms, which might be critical for navigating lifestyles's complexities and accomplishing holistic fulfilment.

In fact, each time management and thought control are complementary and interconnected. achievement regularly requires a balance between powerful time utilisation and emotional resilience. While time management helps people acquire particular responsibilities and desires correctly, thought control equips them with the mental assets to address setbacks, adapt to alternate, and preserve properly-being amidst challenges.

Ultimately, the combination of both time and thoughts management strategies is fundamental to attaining sustainable success and fulfilment in life. Through efficiently coping with time and nurturing intellectual fitness, people can create a basis for success that encompasses productivity, resilience, and overall proper-being.

Chapter 1:

Understanding the mind-domestic Connection

1) Exploring the hyperlink among intellectual litter and bodily muddle:-

The link between mental clutter and physical litter is a captivating element of human psychology and behaviour, losing light on the profound ways in which our external environments reflect and affect our internal states. This connection highlights the problematic courting among our bodily environment and our mental well-being, underscoring the significance of making harmonious spaces for most useful dwelling.

At its centre, intellectual clutter refers to the accumulation of thoughts, emotions, and cognitive distractions that muddle our minds and hinder readability, consciousness, and peace of thoughts. It encompasses a number of mental phenomena, along with strain, tension, weigh down, and cognitive overload. Mental litter can appear in diverse forms, along with racing thoughts, persistent concerns, and an incapacity to pay attention or make decisions efficiently.

Furthermore, bodily litter refers to the buildup of material possessions, assets, and gadgets within our living spaces that make contributions to disorganisation, chaos, and visible noise. It includes cluttered countertops, overflowing closets, crowded rooms, and immoderate possessions that detract from the capability and aesthetics of our houses. bodily clutter can create feelings of crush, frustration, and dissatisfaction, making it hard to relax, focus, or sense at ease in our own environments.

The link between intellectual clutter and physical clutter lies in their reciprocal relationship:

Every can exacerbate and strengthen the opposite, growing a vicious cycle of disorganisation and distress. whilst our bodily spaces are cluttered and chaotic, it may make a contribution to emotions of mental litter and crush, leading to expanded pressure, tension, and cognitive strain. Conversely, while our minds are cluttered with issues, distractions, and bad mind, it may spill over into our physical environments, manifesting as clutter and disarray.

expertise this connection is fundamental to addressing each intellectual and bodily clutter efficiently. By recognizing the methods wherein our outside surroundings replicate and influence our internal states, we are able to take proactive steps to declutter and simplify our lives, selling more clarity, calm, and nicely-being.

Realistic techniques for exploring the hyperlink between intellectual litter and bodily litter encompass:

Aware focus:
Cultivating mindfulness and self-recognition to understand the methods in which mental muddle and bodily muddle show up in our lives.

Decluttering Practices:
imposing decluttering techniques and organising techniques to streamline our physical environments and reduce visual and spatial muddle.

Emotional release:
Processing and releasing emotional clutter via journaling, meditation, remedy, or other therapeutic modalities to sell emotional nicely-being and resilience.

Developing Sacred areas:
Designating areas within our homes as sacred areas for rest, meditation, and rejuvenation, free from the distractions of litter and chaos.
Cultivating Gratitude: Cultivating gratitude and appreciation for the abundance and benefits in our lives, transferring our reputation from shortage to abundance.

Through the way of exploring the link among intellectual litter and bodily clutter, we are able to embark on an adventure of self-discovery, increase, and transformation, reclaiming our areas and our minds in pursuit of more clarity, peace, and achievement.

Chapter 1:
2) Recognizing How your private home environment affects Your mental nicely-being

Bodily comfort:

A relaxed and beneficial living area that meets our basic goals for safe haven, protection, and comfort fosters an experience of safety and well-being. elements including temperature, lighting, noise ranges, and ergonomic design can all affect our mood and emotional United states.

Company and Order:

An prepared and clutter-unfastened home environment promotes a sense of calm, clarity, and management, lowering emotions of strain, tension, and crush. Conversely, disorganisation and clutter can create visible and intellectual chaos, most important to feelings of frustration and dissatisfaction.

Aesthetic appeal:

The aesthetic attraction of our domestic environment—which incorporates coloration schemes, decor, and design elements—can evoke superb emotions, encourage creativity, and uplift our spirits. Surrounding ourselves with beauty and giant objects that resonate with our personal tastes and values can beautify our general experience of proper-being.

Capability and waft:
A well-designed and useful domestic format that enables our daily activities and physical activities promotes efficiency, productivity, and an experience of ease in navigating our living areas. A lack of functionality or obstructed flow can bring about feelings of frustration and restriction.

Emotional environment:
The emotional surroundings inner our domestic, which incorporates the tremendous of relationships, communication patterns, and emotional dynamics, significantly influences our mental fitness and interpersonal interactions. A supportive and nurturing home surroundings characterised through love, recognition, and empathy fosters emotional resilience and pleasant social connections.

spotting how our home environment affects our intellectual well-being empowers us to make intentional options and adjustments to create areas that nurture and assist our mental fitness and happiness. By prioritising consolation, organisation, aesthetic attraction, capability, and emotional concord inside our houses, we can cultivate environments that sell resilience, positivity, and common well-being for ourselves and our cherished ones.

Realistic steps for spotting and improving the impact of our home environment on our highbrow nicely-being may additionally include decluttering and organising areas, incorporating factors of nature and herbal light, developing particular areas for rest and rejuvenation, fostering open and supportive conversation with circle of relatives individuals, and in search of expert assist or guidance at the same time as wished.

In the long run, by means of cultivating conscious cognizance and intentional layout standards inside our houses, we are able to rework our residing spaces into sanctuaries of well-being and sanctuary, nurturing our intellectual health and enriching our everyday lives with that means, motive, and pleasure.

Chapter 2:

The power of Time thinking

1) Introducing the idea of Time questioning:

Time thinking is a transformative concept that gives a fresh angle on how we understand and manipulate time in our everyday lives. Unlike traditional time management strategies that focus entirely on productivity and performance, Time thinking emphasises a holistic and aware technique to time utilisation, prioritisation, and purpose attainment. At its middle, Time questioning encourages people to domesticate a deeper focus and appreciation of the present second, even as additionally strategically making plans for the destiny and studying from the beyond.

Central to the concept of Time wandering is the popularity that point is not simply an aid to be controlled, but a treasured and finite aspect of our lives that merits our interest, intention, and recognition. In preference to viewing time as a continuing taskmaster or a supply of strain and stress, Time thinking invites us to reframe our relationship with time as a source of opportunity, creativity, and opportunity.

Key principles of Time wondering include:

Present second consciousness:

Embracing the energy of mindfulness and giving second awareness to fully interact with the right here and now. by grounding ourselves inside the present moment, we are able to cultivate a feel of readability, calm, and purpose in our movements and decisions.

Strategic planning:

Taking a proactive and intentional approach to time control with the aid of setting clear goals, priorities, and objectives. Time questioning encourages people to become aware of their values, passions, and long-term aspirations, and to align their every day sports and commitments consequently.

Flexibility and adaptability:

Recognizing the fluid and dynamic nature of time and being open to adjusting plans and expectations as instances exchange. Time questioning emphasises the significance of pliability, resilience, and adaptability in navigating the complexities of lifestyles and paintings.

Mirrored image and gaining knowledge of:

Incorporating regular intervals of reflection and self-evaluation to evaluate our use of time, perceive regions for development, and celebrate achievements. By embracing a boom mindset and a willingness to analyse from both successes and setbacks, we can constantly refine our approach to time management and private increase.

Balance and well-being:

Prioritising stability and well-being in our pursuit of productiveness and success. Time thinking recognizes the significance of rest, rest, and self-care as essential additives of a healthy and pleasing lifestyle. by honouring our need for downtime and renewal, we can maintain our strength, creativity, and resilience over the long time.

imposing the ideas of Time questioning requires a shift in mindset and behaviour, as well as a dedication to cultivating new habits and exercises. It includes letting go of perfectionism and embracing imperfection, trusting in the procedure of boom and transformation, and being gentle and compassionate with ourselves alongside the manner.

Sensible techniques for incorporating Time questioning into our lives might also encompass:

Placing apart dedicated time for reflection, journaling, and aim putting.
growing day by day, weekly, and month-to-month schedules that replicate our values and priorities.

setting up barriers and saying no to activities that don't align with our desires and values.
Embracing moments of relaxation, relaxation, and rejuvenation to refill our power and creativity.

Cultivating a feeling of gratitude and appreciation for the gift of time and the possibilities it gives us.

By embracing the concepts of Time questioning, we will cultivate a deeper feel of achievement, motive, and joy in our lives, while also making significant contributions to the world around us. Time wandering invites us to reclaim possession of our time and to live with intention, authenticity, and presence in each second.

Chapter 2:
2. "Understanding How Time thinking Can rework your private home and thoughts"

Time thinking represents an effective paradigm shift in how we perceive and engage with time, providing profound implications for both our home environments and our mental well-being. Through embracing the standards of Time thinking, people can free up new levels of productiveness, achievement, and concord of their lives, fostering an experience of reason and empowerment that transcends traditional tactics to time control.

At its centre, Time wandering invites us to reframe our dating with time as a dynamic and fluid resource that can be harnessed and leveraged to enhance each of our domestic environments and our inner landscapes. By cultivating a deeper consciousness and appreciation of the existing moment, whilst also strategically making plans for the future and reflecting on the beyond, Time thinking empowers us to stay with purpose, mindfulness, and motive in each thing of our lives.

Key elements of the way Time questioning can rework your private home and thoughts include:

Clarity and attention:

Via adopting a Time wandering mind-set, individuals can gain extra clarity and focus of their each day activities and priorities.

Through figuring out their middle values, goals, and aspirations, they are able to align their movements and selections with their genuine priorities, leading to a greater functional and pleasurable lifestyle.

Efficiency and productivity:

Time questioning encourages people to optimise their use of time through prioritising duties, setting sensible cut-off dates, and minimising distractions. By cultivating habits of field, business enterprise, and cognizance, individuals can maximise their productiveness and achieve more with less effort, releasing up time for sports that carry joy and success.

Strain reduction and well-being:

By embracing the ideas of Time questioning, individuals can reduce feelings of stress, weigh down, and tension associated with time control demanding situations. With the aid of adopting a proactive and intentional approach to time control, they are able to create an experience of order, manipulation, and stability in their lives, leading to more peace of thoughts and emotional well-being.

Creativity and Innovation:

Time thinking fosters an environment of creativity and innovation by way of encouraging people to discover new thoughts, test with one-of-a-kind methods, and embody failure as a natural part of gaining knowledge of method. by giving themselves permission to think outside the field and take calculated risks, individuals can release new degrees of creativity and problem-fixing capability.

Connection and Relationships:

With the aid of prioritising high-quality time with cherished ones and fostering significant connections, Time questioning helps people support their relationships and deepen their sense of belonging and network. With the aid of carving out devoted time for bonding, conversation, and shared studies, individuals can nurture the bonds that increase their lives and sustain them through existence's challenges.

Realistic techniques for enforcing Time wondering in your private home and mind might also encompass:

organising each day exercises and rituals that sell mindfulness and intentionality.
developing committed areas within your home for mirrored image, rest, and rejuvenation.
placing a part time for planning, goal placing, and self-assessment on a regular basis.
Cultivating habits of gratitude, appreciation, and mindfulness to your daily interactions and sports.

Embracing moments of stillness and solitude to recharge your power and reconnect along with your inner know-how.
With the aid of embracing the transformative energy of Time questioning, individuals can release new degrees of creativity, productiveness, and success in their lives, developing homes and minds that are aligned with their real values and aspirations. Time wondering invitations us to reclaim possession of our time and to stay with purpose, passion, and presence in each moment.

Chapter 2:

3) Gaining knowledge of to Prioritise responsibilities and control Time effectively

Mastering to prioritise tasks and control time efficiently is a fundamental talent that empowers individuals to make the maximum in their to be had time, accomplish their goals, and hold an experience of balance and success in their lives. In a world characterised with the aid of regular needs and distractions, learning this talent is essential for navigating the complexities of labour, home, and personal responsibilities with grace and efficiency.

At its centre, effective task prioritisation and time management contain identifying your maximum essential goals, allocating it slowly and resources as a consequence, and maintaining a focus on excessive-impact activities that align together with your overarching goals and values. via adopting strategic planning strategies, cultivating, and embracing a proactive mind-set, individuals can conquer procrastination, decrease strain, and maximise their productiveness and delight in both professional and private domain names.

Key factors of gaining knowledge of to prioritise obligations and manage time efficaciously consist of:

Figuring out Priorities: step one in effective time control is figuring out your priorities and dreams. by clarifying what subjects are maximum to you and aligning your activities along with your values and aspirations, you could make certain that your slowness and strength are directed toward significant pastimes that make contributions to your long-term success and fulfilment.

Placing clear goals:
Putting clean, particular, and doable targets is essential for effective undertaking prioritisation and time management. By breaking down large goals into smaller, actionable steps, you may create a roadmap for fulfilment and keep a sense of momentum and development to your endeavours.

Creating a flexible agenda:
While having an agenda is essential for staying organised and on track, it's also critical to remain flexible and adaptable inside the face of surprising adjustments and challenges. through building in buffer time and bearing in mind contingencies, you may better navigate disruptions and hold a feel of control over it slowly and priorities.

Making use of Time blocking off:
Time blocking off is a powerful method for structuring your day and optimising your productivity. by allocating specific blocks of time to focus on key obligations and tasks, you can limit distractions, preserve a feel of momentum, and make big development toward your goals.

Working towards is an essential factor of effective time management. By means of cultivating behaviour of attention, diligence, and endurance, you could overcome procrastination, withstand temptations, and stay devoted to your priorities even if confronted with demanding situations and distractions.

Imposing systems and tools:
Leveraging productivity structures and equipment can streamline your workflow and decorate your efficiency. Whether or not it is the use of virtual calendars, challenge management apps, or project monitoring software programs, finding gear that align with your alternatives and workflow allow you to live organised and on pinnacle of your obligations.

Reflecting and Adjusting:
Frequently reflecting on your progress and adjusting your method as needed is essential for continuous improvement in time control. By comparing what is running properly and what could be advanced, you can refine your strategies, optimise your workflow, and adapt to converting instances more efficiently.

Realistic strategies for mastering to prioritise responsibilities and manage time efficiently may additionally encompass:

Engaging in a regular review of your desires and priorities to make sure alignment together with your values and aspirations.
Breaking down large tasks into smaller, greater achievable chunks to facilitate progress and decrease weight.

Prioritising duties based totally on their urgency, importance, and potential effect on your long-term desires.

placing aside dedicated time for centred paintings and minimising interruptions and distractions throughout these durations.

looking for assistance and responsibility from mentors, coaches, or friends that will help you stay on course and conquer limitations.

By using getting to know to prioritise obligations and manage time successfully, individuals can manage their schedules, reduce strain, and create more area for the activities and relationships that convey joy and fulfilment to their lives. With determination, exercise, and a commitment to continuous improvement, learning this ability can release new ranges of productivity, delight, and achievement in each expert and personal domain names.

Chapter 3:

Overcoming worry and anxiety :-

1) Figuring out assets of fear and anxiety in your property and mind

Know-how the resources of fear and tension in your private home and mind is a vital step towards addressing and handling these tough feelings efficiently. In an ultra-modern fast-paced and traumatic world, it's not unusual for individuals to experience feelings of pressure and tension stemming from various elements of their environment, way of life, and inner thoughts. By identifying the specific triggers and underlying causes of fear and anxiety, people can develop centred techniques for coping, resilience, and emotional nicely-being.

Outside Stressors:
External stressors inside the domestic surroundings can contribute to emotions of fear and tension. Those might also include financial concerns, work-related pressures, courting conflicts, fitness troubles, or other existence challenges that affect day by day existence. With the aid of spotting the specific stressors which might be present in your house surroundings, you may start to deal with them proactively and are looking for aid or assets to manipulate them more efficiently.

Bodily clutter and Disorganization:
Muddle and disorganisation inside the domestic can create a sense of crush and make a contribution to emotions of anxiety. While living areas are cluttered and chaotic, it may be difficult to relax, be aware, or discover peace of thoughts. With the aid of identifying areas of litter and implementing techniques for decluttering and employer, individuals can create an extra harmonious and calming surroundings that supports their intellectual nice-being.

Bad behaviour and lifestyle alternatives:
Dangerous conduct and life-style alternatives, including terrible vitamins, lack of workout, inadequate sleep, or excessive display time, can exacerbate emotions of anxiety and strain. by recognizing patterns of conduct that may be contributing to your emotional misery, you can make intentional changes to prioritise self-care, balance, and universal proper-being.

Bad notion styles:
Terrible thought styles and cognitive distortions can gasoline emotions of fear and anxiety inside the thoughts. These might also encompass catastrophizing, overgeneralizing, black-and-white wandering, or excessive rumination on beyond activities or destiny uncertainties. By becoming aware of those idea patterns and their validity, people can domesticate an extra balanced and realistic perspective that promotes resilience and mental fitness.

Perfectionism and Unrealistic expectancies:
Perfectionism and unrealistic expectations also can be resources of worry and anxiety, mainly whilst individuals sense stress to meet impossibly excessive standards or gain inconceivable dreams.

with the aid of acknowledging the restrictions of perfectionism and embracing a mind-set of self-compassion and attractiveness, people can reduce feelings of strain and domesticate a greater experience of peace and success in their lives.

Environmental Stressors:

Environmental stressors, such as noise pollution, air pollutants, or publicity to virtual devices, can impact intellectual well-being and make contributions to emotions of tension. through figuring out environmental factors that can be triggering or exacerbating your anxiety, you could take steps to limit publicity and create an extra supportive and nurturing residing environment.

Sensible techniques for figuring out sources of fear and anxiety in your own home and thoughts may additionally include:

Keeping a mag to music sorts of thoughts, feelings, and behaviours that contribute to emotions of hysteria.
undertaking mindfulness practices, such as meditation or deep breathing sports, to cultivate present-second awareness and reduce stress.
in search of support from trusted friends, own family people, or intellectual fitness experts to explore and deal with underlying issues contributing to anxiety.
developing a supportive and nurturing domestic surroundings that promotes relaxation, tranquillity, and emotional proper-being.

Through taking proactive steps to pick out and address sources of worry and anxiety in your own home and mind, you could cultivate resilience, emotional balance, and an extra sense of peace and achievement to your everyday lifestyles. via the usage of acknowledging and honouring your emotional critiques, you could embark on an adventure of self-discovery and boom that leads to more readability, resilience, and well-being.

Chapter 3:

2) Implementing strategies to manipulate and reduce tension stages

Mastering to prioritise tasks and control time efficiently is a fundamental talent that empowers individuals to make the maximum in their to be had time, accomplish their goals, and hold an experience of balance and success in their lives. In a world characterised with the aid of regular needs and distractions, learning this talent is essential for navigating the complexities of labour, home, and personal responsibilities with grace and efficiency.

At its centre, effective task prioritisation and time management contain identifying your maximum essential goals, allocating it slowly and resources as a consequence, and maintaining a focus on excessive-impact activities that align together with your overarching goals and values. via adopting strategic planning strategies, cultivating, and embracing a proactive mind-set, individuals can conquer procrastination, decrease strain, and maximise their productiveness and delight in both professional and private domain names.

Key factors of gaining knowledge of to prioritise obligations and manage time efficaciously consist of:

Figuring out Priorities:

Step one in effective time control is figuring out your priorities and dreams. by clarifying what subjects are maximum to you and aligning your activities along with your values and aspirations, you could make certain that your slowness and strength are directed toward significant pastimes that make contributions to your long-term success and fulfilment.

Placing clear goals:

Putting clean, particular, and doable targets is essential for effective undertaking prioritisation and time management. By breaking down large goals into smaller, actionable steps, you may create a roadmap for fulfilment and keep a sense of momentum and development to your endeavours.

Creating a flexible agenda:

While having an agenda is essential for staying organised and on track, it's also critical to remain flexible and adaptable inside the face of surprising adjustments and challenges. through building in buffer time and bearing in mind contingencies, you may better navigate disruptions and hold a feel of control over it slowly and priorities.

Making use of Time blocking off:

Time blocking off is a powerful method for structuring your day and optimising your productivity. by allocating specific blocks of time to focus on key obligations and tasks, you can limit distractions, preserve a feel of momentum, and make big development toward your goals.

Working towards is an essential factor of effective time management. By means of cultivating behaviour of attention, diligence, and endurance, you could overcome procrastination, withstand temptations, and stay devoted to your priorities even if confronted with demanding situations and distractions.

Imposing systems and tools: Leveraging productivity structures and equipment can streamline your workflow and decorate your efficiency. Whether or not it is the use of virtual calendars, challenge management apps, or project monitoring software programs, finding gear that align with your alternatives and workflow allow you to live organised and on pinnacle of your obligations.

Reflecting and Adjusting: frequently reflecting on your progress and adjusting your method as needed is essential for continuous improvement in time control. By comparing what is running properly and what could be advanced, you can refine your strategies, optimise your workflow, and adapt to converting instances more efficiently.

Realistic strategies for mastering to prioritise responsibilities and manage time efficiently may additionally encompass:

Engaging in a regular review of your desires and priorities to make sure alignment together with your values and aspirations.
Breaking down large tasks into smaller, greater achievable chunks to facilitate progress and decrease weight.

Prioritising duties based totally on their urgency, importance, and potential effect on your long-term desires.
placing aside dedicated time for centred paintings and minimising interruptions and distractions throughout these durations.
looking for assistance and responsibility from mentors, coaches, or friends that will help you stay on course and conquer limitations.
By using getting to know to prioritise obligations and manage time successfully, individuals can manage their schedules, reduce strain, and create more area for the activities and relationships that convey joy and fulfilment to their lives. With determination, exercise, and a commitment to continuous improvement, learning this ability can release new ranges of productivity, delight, and achievement in each expert and personal domain names.

Chapter 3:

3) Cultivating Mindfulness Practices to stay gift and Calm

Know-how the resources of fear and tension in your private home and mind is a vital step towards addressing and handling these tough feelings efficiently. In an ultra-modern fast-paced and traumatic world, it's not unusual for individuals to experience feelings of pressure and tension stemming from various elements of their environment, way of life, and inner thoughts. By identifying the specific triggers and underlying causes of fear and anxiety, people can develop centred techniques for coping, resilience, and emotional nicely-being.

Outside Stressors:

External stressors inside the domestic surroundings can contribute to emotions of fear and tension. Those might also include financial concerns, work-related pressures, courting conflicts, fitness troubles, or other existence challenges that affect day by day existence. With the aid of spotting the specific stressors which might be present in your house surroundings, you may start to deal with them proactively and are looking for aid or assets to manipulate them more efficiently.

Bodily clutter and Disorganization:

Muddle and disorganisation inside the domestic can create a sense of crush and make a contribution to emotions of anxiety. While living areas are cluttered and chaotic, it may be difficult to relax, be aware, or discover peace of thoughts. With the aid of identifying areas of litter and implementing techniques for decluttering and employer, individuals can create an extra harmonious and calming surroundings that supports their intellectual nice-being.

Bad behaviour and lifestyle alternatives:

Dangerous conduct and life-style alternatives, including terrible vitamins, lack of workout, inadequate sleep, or excessive display time, can exacerbate emotions of anxiety and strain. by recognizing patterns of conduct that may be contributing to your emotional misery, you can make intentional changes to prioritise self-care, balance, and universal proper-being.

Bad notion styles:

Terrible thought styles and cognitive distortions can gasoline emotions of fear and anxiety inside the thoughts. These might also encompass catastrophizing, overgeneralizing, black-and-white wandering, or excessive rumination on beyond activities or destiny uncertainties. By becoming aware of those idea patterns and their validity, people can domesticate an extra balanced and realistic perspective that promotes resilience and mental fitness.

Perfectionism and Unrealistic expectancies:

Perfectionism and unrealistic expectations also can be resources of worry and anxiety, mainly whilst individuals sense stress to meet impossibly excessive standards or gain inconceivable dreams. with the aid of acknowledging the restrictions of perfectionism and embracing a mind-set of self-compassion and attractiveness, people can reduce feelings of strain and domesticate a greater experience of peace and success in their lives.

Environmental Stressors:

Environmental stressors, such as noise pollution, air pollutants, or publicity to virtual devices, can impact intellectual well-being and make contributions to emotions of tension. through figuring out environmental factors that can be triggering or exacerbating your anxiety, you could take steps to limit publicity and create an extra supportive and nurturing residing environment.

Sensible techniques for figuring out sources of fear and anxiety in your own home and thoughts may additionally include:

Keeping a mag to music sorts of thoughts, feelings, and behaviours that contribute to emotions of hysteria. undertaking mindfulness practices, such as meditation or deep breathing sports, to cultivate present-second awareness and reduce stress.

in search of support from trusted friends, own family people, or intellectual fitness experts to explore and deal with underlying issues contributing to anxiety.

Developing a supportive and nurturing domestic surroundings that promotes relaxation, tranquillity, and emotional proper-being.

Through taking proactive steps to pick out and address sources of worry and anxiety in your own home and mind, you could cultivate resilience, emotional balance, and an extra sense of peace and achievement to your everyday lifestyles. via the usage of acknowledging and honouring your emotional critiques, you could embark on an adventure of self-discovery and boom that leads to more readability, resilience, and well-being.

"Enforcing techniques to manipulate and decrease tension ranges"

Tension can be a debilitating emotion that influences diverse components of our lives, from our relationships and paintings performance to our universal well-being and niceness of life. However, by imposing effective strategies to manage and reduce tension ranges, individuals can regain a sense of control, resilience, and peace of mind. Those techniques contain a mixture of practical strategies, way of life changes, and therapeutic interventions designed to cope with the root reasons of hysteria and domesticate emotional nicely-being.

Mindfulness and relaxation strategies:

Mindfulness practices, such as meditation, deep respiration physical activities, and innovative muscle relaxation, can assist individuals calm their minds, reduce physical tension, and cultivate gift-moment attention. By incorporating these techniques into their every day recurring, individuals can broaden more resilience to strain and anxiety even as promoting a sense of calm and stability.

Healthy lifestyle habits:

Engaging in ordinary bodily pastime, maintaining a balanced eating regimen, prioritising adequate sleep, and minimising the intake of stimulants like caffeine and alcohol are crucial components of coping with anxiety levels. workout releases endorphins, which can be herbal temper enhancers, while a nutritious diet and sufficient sleep guide usual physical and mental nicely-being, reducing susceptibility to tension.

Cognitive-Behavioural strategies:

Cognitive-behavioural remedy (CBT) is a widely recognized healing technique for handling anxiety. by using identifying and hard terrible notion patterns and replacing them with extra balanced and practical ideals, individuals can lessen anxiety signs and expand healthier coping strategies. CBT additionally consists of behavioural strategies which include exposure therapy and systematic desensitisation to help people confront and conquer tension triggers step by step.

Pressure control techniques:

Getting to know to correctly manipulate stress can drastically reduce anxiety levels. strategies which include time control, assertive communique, trouble-fixing abilities, and setting limitations can assist people navigate stressors greater successfully and build resilience to anxiety-provoking situations. relaxation activities such as yoga, tai chi, and guided imagery also can sell relaxation and stress reduction.

Social support and Connection:

Retaining strong social connections and searching for guidance from buddies, circle of relatives contributors, or aid groups can offer valuable emotional assistance and angle at some stage in times of heightened tension. Sharing stories, expressing feelings, and receiving validation from others can assist people experience understanding and much less remote in their struggles with anxiety.

Professional help and remedy:

In some cases, professional intervention can be necessary to correctly manipulate anxiety.

Therapists, counsellors, and psychiatrists can offer proof-primarily based treatments consisting of cognitive-behavioural remedy, remedy, or an aggregate of each, tailored to the man or woman's unique needs and instances. seeking expert assistance is a proactive step towards addressing anxiety and enhancing common intellectual health.

Self-Care and strain reduction activities:

conducting activities that promote relaxation, creativity, and self-expression may be effective antidotes to tension. Pursuits which include artwork, tune, gardening, or spending time in nature can offer a feel of pleasure and achievement at the same time as imparting a reprieve from stressful mind and emotions.

Mindfulness-based total Interventions:

Mindfulness-primarily based interventions, including mindfulness-based strain discount (MBSR) and reputation and dedication remedy (ACT), incorporate mindfulness practices into therapeutic strategies to help people broaden popularity, resilience, and psychological flexibility inside the face of tension. Those interventions emphasise being present with difficult feelings and mastering to respond to them with compassion and self-attention.

implementing techniques to manage and reduce tension ranges requires dedication, patience, and self-compassion. By taking proactive steps to deal with tension via a mixture of way of life changes, healing strategies, and social help, individuals can cultivate extra resilience, emotional stability, and proper-being in their lives. Recognizing that coping with anxiety is a journey, no longer a destination, individuals can embrace the manner of self-discovery and increase, finding power and empowerment of their capacity to navigate existence's demanding situations with courage and resilience.

"Cultivating Mindfulness Practices to stay gift and Calm"

IIn latest speedy-paced global, cultivating mindfulness practices has turned out to be more and more crucial for humans looking to discover peace, clarity, and stability amidst the chaos of regular life. Mindfulness entails the exercising of intentionally focusing one's attention on the present 2nd, with a mind-set of openness, hobby, and non-judgment. with the aid of cultivating mindfulness practices, humans can enlarge more self-cognizance, emotional law, and resilience, in the end most important to a deeper revel in calm, presence, and proper-being.

Cognizance of the Breath:
one of the foundational practices of mindfulness involves being attentive to the breath. by means of focusing on the sensations of the breath as it enters and leaves the frame, human beings can anchor themselves in the gift 2d, cultivating a feel of internal calm and groundedness.

Body test Meditation:
Frame test meditation involves systematically scanning the body from head to toe, listening to any sensations, tensions, or regions of soreness. This exercise helps people increase extra attention of bodily sensations and promotes rest and release of bodily anxiety.

Conscious movement:

Aware movement practices, such as yoga, tai chi, or on foot meditation, contain transferring the frame with purpose and cognizance. With the aid of syncing movement with breath and taking note of the sensations of the body, individuals can cultivate a feel of ease, grace, and embodied presence.

Observing mind and emotions:

Mindfulness encourages individuals to examine their thoughts and emotions with interest and non-judgmental recognition. As opposed to getting caught up inside the content material of mind or looking to suppress or control feelings, humans discover ways to look at them as passing phenomena, allowing them to come and pass without attachment or resistance.

Bringing cognizance to each day's sports activities:

Mindfulness can be infused into normal sports, such as consuming, cooking, cleansing, or walking. Through bringing an entire hobby and presence to those sports, people can redecorate mundane tasks into possibilities for mirrored image, connection, and gratitude.

Mindfulness in communique:

Aware verbal exchange includes listening deeply to others with complete interest and empathy, without judgement or distraction. Through being completely observed in conversations and expressing oneself with authenticity and readability, human beings can foster deeper connections and data of their relationships.

Running towards Non-reactivity and popularity:

Mindfulness encourages people to cultivate a mind-set of non-reactivity and popularity toward their internal experiences and outdoor instances. In place of resisting or combating in competition to tough feelings or hard conditions, people learn how to meet them with compassion, staying power, and equanimity.

Formal Meditation exercise:

Wearing out formal meditation exercise, which include sitting meditation or loving-kindness meditation, provides established possibilities to cultivate mindfulness and deepen one's practice. Through putting aside dedicated time for meditation, people can help their attentional abilities, develop emotional resilience, and cultivate a feel of inner peace and proper-being.

Incorporating mindfulness practices into everyday life requires determination, staying power, and regular try. With the resources of integrating these practices into everyday workout routines and sports, humans can regularly domesticate a deeper experience of presence, calm, and readability of their lives. In the long run, mindfulness isn't always simply a way or exercise, however a way of being—a profound shift in attitude that invites humans to encompass each moment with openness, interest, and gratitude, finding splendour and meaning in the smooth act of being alive.

Chapter 4:

Streamlining your private home surroundings:-

1) Simplifying Your residing area without Decluttering Your thoughts

Inside the modern-day world, where our lives are regularly packed with busyness, distractions, and overwhelming needs, the idea of simplifying our dwelling area without decluttering our minds has received great importance. Simplification involves streamlining our bodily surroundings and lifestyle to create an experience of spaciousness, tranquillity, and harmony, without including the intellectual burden of decluttering our minds.

Intentional design:

Simplifying your dwelling space begins with intentional layout. by cautiously selecting furniture, decorations, and belongings that serve a cause and bring pleasure, you could create a minimalist aesthetic that promotes calmness and clarity.

Clearing physical muddle:

Even as simplifying your living area would not always suggest decluttering your mind, it regularly entails clearing bodily clutter. Putting off extra property, organising garage areas, and prioritising critical items can create an experience of openness and simplicity in your property environment.

Embracing Minimalism:

Embracing minimalism is a key element of simplifying your living space. Minimalism encourages individuals to recognize the best over quantity, emphasising simplicity, functionality, and aesthetic splendour of their environment.

Developing purposeful Zones:

Simplifying your living area entails creating purposeful zones for different activities and purposes. by using delineating regions for relaxation, paintings, socialising, and self-care, you can optimise the drift and usefulness of your living area.

Mindful consumption:

conscious intake is crucial for simplifying your residing space without adding to intellectual muddle. by being intentional about what you bring into your property, you could avoid useless purchases and reduce the accumulation of assets that make a contribution to overwhelm and disorganisation.

Virtual Detox:

Simplifying your residing space extends in your virtual surroundings as nicely. do not forget imposing a virtual detox by way of decreasing display time, decluttering virtual gadgets, and growing limitations around era use to promote intellectual readability and presence.

Prioritising relaxation and rest:

Simplifying your living area method prioritising rest and relaxation. Create cosy nooks, secure seating regions, and serene bedroom environments that invite restorative rest and rejuvenation.

Practising Mindfulness:

Mindfulness practices can help simplify your living area by selling focus, presence, and popularity of the existing moment. have interaction in mindful sports which include meditation, yoga, or nature walks to domesticate a sense of calm and reference to your environment.

Letting go of Perfectionism:

Simplifying your residing space calls for letting go of perfectionism and embracing imperfection. accept that your private home won't always be photograph-best, and awareness alternatively on creating an surroundings that helps your proper-being and displays your values and priorities.

Cultivating Gratitude:

Cultivating gratitude is a powerful way to simplify your living space and declutter your mind. Take time every day to comprehend the splendour and abundance for your environment, expressing gratitude for the easy pleasures and benefits to your life.

In the end, simplifying your living area without decluttering your mind is ready to grow an environment that nurtures your nice-being, fosters tranquillity, and helps a balanced lifestyle. By embracing intentional design, minimalism, mindful intake, and gratitude, you may cultivate a residing area that feels spacious, serene, and authentically yours, without adding to the mental clutter of contemporary lifestyles.

Chapter 4:

2) Sensible suggestions for Organizing and keeping a clutter-free home

Msbuild Integrated a clutter-loose domestic is not handiest visually attractive integrated but additionally contributes to an experience of calm, employer, and properly-be built-in. built-in built-in integrated sensible built-in integrated for organic integrated and built-inbuilt integrated a litter-free home, built-in can create a harmonious reidbuilt integrated environment integrated that promotes productiveness, relaxation, and peace of thoughts integrated.

Declutter often:

Integrated by us built integrated declutter integrated your own home regularly to built-innate objects which are now not wished or used. start with one location at a time, together with closets, integrated, or drawers, built-in integrated through built-in assets to perceive gadgets to donate, promote, or discard.

Set up Organisational structures:

Establish organisational structures to built-in integrated belongbuilt integrated built-in order and easily available. built-in storage answers built-in integrated baskets, canbuilt integrated, and drawer dividers to categorise and shop items efficiently.

Designate garage areas:
Designate particular garage areas for distbuilt integrated categories of gadgets, built-in integrated built-in apparel, footwear, accessories, household materials, and paperwork. simply label garage built-ins and built-in to facilitate smooth identification and retrieval of gadgets.

Create every day exercises:
set up day by day routines for tidybuilt-ing up and built integrated a clutter-free domestic. Spend built-in integrated every day declutter integrated surfaces, built-in integrated away built-in, and return integrated items to their targeted storage areas to prevent muddle from amass built integrated.

Exercise the "One In, One Out" Rule:
undertake the "one built-in, one out" rule to prevent new muddle from built-in integrated your property. For every new object added built-into the house, decide to build-ing off a comparable object to built-i keep a balanced and clutter-free built-in.

Stream Built-in paperwork:
manipulate paperwork and documents efficiently by means of sorts integrated thru mail, bills, and office work regularly. built-in integrated a built-infill built integrated gadget or digital corporation tools to preserve integrated critical documents prepared and effortlessly available.

Maximise Vertical space:

Employ a vertical area to maximise storage and integrated muddle. deploy cab built integrated, hooks, and peg boards on walls to save objects built-in integrated books, kitchen utensils, and ornamental accents, built-in integrated up valuable floor area.

Limit decorative Accents:

While decorative accents can add character and warmth to a home, keep away from overcrowd integrated surfaces with too many decorative objects. pick out some built-inmean built integrated pieces that built-ing joy and complement your private home's aesthetic, and rotate them periodically to built-intabuild integrated the gap feel integrated clean and uncluttered.

Built-in integrated Multi-functional fixtures:

choose multi-purposeful fixtures portions that serve built-in purposes, along with garage ottomans, espresso tables with storage, and beds with under-mattress drawers. Those fixtures pieces help maximise space and built-in built integrated litter built-in smaller built-in regions.

Built-inary protection and evaluation:

Time table everyday integrated upkeep classes to study and built-in integrated your organisational systems and declutter integrated efforts. Take time to evaluate what is integrated nicely and what might be progressed, and make changes as hard to integrate a litter-free domestic surround built.

by integrated practical built-ins for organic integrated and built-in a clutter-unfastened domestic, built-in can create a space that feels built-invite integrated, serene, and conducive to their usual properly-be built-in. With constant effort and mint gratefulness, built-in integrated litter-unfastened homes will become a sustainable integrated way of life dependency that integrated joy, peace, and harmony to daily built-in integration.

Chapter 4:

3) Growing functional and pressure-unfastened residing areas

Our built-ing areas serve as the heart of our homes, built-in we gather, relax, and connect to cherished ones. built-in practical and built-in-unfastened built-in integrated regions is important for promoting built integrated consolation, ease, and nicely-bebuilt-ing built-in our day by day lives. built-in design integrated those spaces thoughtfully and deliberately, built integrated can domesticate environments that help productivity, relaxation, and harmony.

Compare the layout:

Built-in through integrated the layout of your built-inliv built integrated regions to optimise functionality and flow. built-into account how you operate the space and set up furnishings integrated in a way that helps at ease movement and verbal exchange. built-in integrated pathways are clear and unobstructed to sell ease of motion.

Maximise herbal mild:

Herbal mild has an enormous effect on mood and well-be integrated g. Maximise herbal mild constructed-on your built-in integrated areas built-in integrated built-in unobstructed, built-in integrated sheer curtain integrated built-built-ins or built-in integrated to govern glare, and strategically mirrors to reflect light and create an revel built integrated of spaciousness.

Declutter Surfaces:
Cluttered surfaces can make contributions to integration of built-in and crush. hold surfaces litter-unfastened built-in integrated designatbuilt-ing specific areas for gadgets built-ing of keys, mail, and far off controls. Use decorative baskets or trays to corral smaller objects and create an experience of order and cohesion.

Create Zones for exceptional activities:
Divide your wellbuilt integrated areas built-into zones for extraord built integrated sports, built-ing of long built-in, dining, and enjoyment integrated. Use location rugs, furniture placement, and integrated to delbuilt-ineate those zones and create dist built integrated areas for relaxation, socialise built-in, and productiveness.

Built-in secure Seat Integrated:
Cosy seat built-ing is essential for built-in integratedvitintegratedg and functional built-inlivbuiltintegrated regions. pick seat integrated options that are supportive, cosy, and conducive to relaxation. built-in integrated built-incorporate integrated an expansion of seatbuilt-ing arrangements, which built integrated sofas, armchairs, and ottomans, to house different alternatives and sports.

Integrated garage answers:

Effective storage answers assist ms build constructed built-included wellbuilt built-inbuilt integrated areas organised and clutter-unfastened. built-in built built-in integrated furniture quantities with garage, constructed-built integrated espresso tables with drawers or ottomans with hidden cubicles. Use bookcases, shelf devices, and baskets to build-inbuilt built integrated books, magazine built-built-integrations, and different belonging built integrated built-in integrated out of sight.

Promote Accessibility and Accessibility:

Built-in devices used often are without difficulty accessible and built integrated atta built built-in integrated. store frequently used items without problems reachable
locations and use storage
solutions that promote accessibility, such as pull-out drawers and adjustable shelf integrated. don't forget the needs of all household individuals, built integrated youngsters and built integrated with mobility built-in, whilst design integrated built-in integrated areas.

Built-in integrated non-public Touches:

Personalise your integrated areas with integrated touches that reflect your character and fashion. display loved images, built-in integrated, and mementos that built-in built integrated joy and evoke effective built-iniscences. built-in corporate integrated factors of nature, which built integrated flora and vegetation, to add freshness and vitality to the distance.

Built-in built integrated Distractions:

Built-in distractions built-in your built-ing areas to promote cognizance and rest. built-in electronic gadgets built-in integrated televisions, computers, and smartphones built-in certain areas and establish obstacles round screen time. Create quiet zones for studybuiltintegrated, meditation, and reflection built-in distractions are integrated.

Sell rest and Serenity:

Layout integrated areas to promote relaxation and serenity. Use soft, neutral colorations and herbal substances to create built-in built-in integrated ecosystem integrated. built-in elements of nature, which built integrated door vegetation and water capabilities, to integrate the outdoors built integrated and create an experience of tranquillity.

Built-in useful and stress-integrated-free built-ing regions requires considerate built-ing plans, attention to detail, and built-int on built-in integrated areas that guide the desires and possibilities of built-in built-in habitats. by built-in corporate integrated these built-in built-into the design and enterprise of your built-in integrated regions, you may cultivate environments that foster rest, connection, and we'll-be integrated for yourself and your loved ones.

Chapter 5:

Casting off poor thinking styles:-

1) Recognizing and hard negative thoughts and ideals

Poor built-ins and beliefs could have a profound impact on our built-ings, behaviours, and usually nicely-integrated. recognize built integrated and integrated these terrible styles is an critical step built-in the direction of cultivate built-in a greater tremendous integrated and resilient integrated. via built-in integrated privy to our idea patterns and actively integrated bad beliefs, we can empower ourselves to cultivate extra self-cognizance, emotional balance, and psychological resilience.

Understand built integrated bad thoughts integrated and beliefs:

Negative built integrated ideals are computerised, frequently unconscious styles of question built integrated that integrated our perceptions of ourselves, others, and the arena around us. Those built-in can also stem from past reports, cultural conditions integrated g, or distorted perceptions of truth.

Not unusual built-in poor built-ind:

Poor built-ins can take a lot of paperwork, built-in-includes self-grievance, catastrophize built-in, black-and-white built-in integrated, and overgeneralization. Self-essential thoughts integrated may additionally built-in integrated harsh judgments of oneself, even as catastrophize built-in built-includes imagbuilt-integrated the worst viable consequences integrated a given situation. Black-and-white built-ins built integrated see integrated situations as all right or all horrific, at the same time as overgeneralization built-includes draw integrated broad conclusions primarily based on built-ined proof.

Built-inspott built integrated terrible idea styles:

Step one built-in built-in bad thoughts integrated and ideals is to end up aware of them. take note of your integrated communication and word when the terrible built-ins get up. built-in a journal to report terribly built integrated and the situations or triggers that precede them. by integrated cognizance of your notion styles, you may built-in identify or build integrated subject matters and underlybuilt-ing ideals.

Built-in integrated the Validity of bad built integrated:

Once you have recognized poor built integrated, venture their validity through ask integrated yourself questions built-includes:

Is there evidence to guide this notion?
Are there opportunity factors or built-in interpretations?
Am I viewbuilt-ing the state of affairs built-in a balanced and practical way?
How would I respond to a pal who expressed comparable thoughts?

Built-in integrated poor built-ins with fantastic Affirmations:

Update terribly built integrated with positive affirmations and statements that reflect self-compassion, resilience, and optimism. Affirmations can assist reframe bad ideals and promote an extra effective self-photograph. Repeat affirmations regularly to rebuild integrated built-in beliefs and counteract terrible self-speak.

Cultivate Built-in Self-Compassion and recognition:

Domesticate self-compassion and attractiveness built-in integrated treat integrated yourself with k integratedness, built integrated, and empathy. I apprehend that terribly built integrals are a herbal part of human enjoyment and that everybody experiences self-doubt and insecurity built-in. practice self-care sports together with meditation, integrated mindfulness, and journal integrated to nurture self-compassion and sell emotions nicely-built-in.

Look built integrated guide and angle:

Atta built integrated out to trusted buddies, circle of relatives, individuals, or mental health professionals for guidance and attitude. Discuss Built-ing your poor built integrated beliefs with others can help provide opportunity view built-ins, validation, and encouragement. remedy or counsel integrated can offer additional equipment and techniques for difficult poor thought patterns and integrated resilience.

Training Mintegrateddfulness and cognizance:
Exercise built-mindfulness and present-moment cognizance to exam built integrated bad thoughts integrated without judgement or attachment. be aware whilst negative built integrated get up and lightly redirect your attention to the prevail built integrated second. Built-mindfulness strategies along with deep built-in, frame scans, and guided imagery can assist cultivate a feel of calm and detachment from negative notion styles.

Foster Integrated a built integrated built-in:
Embrace a built-in increase integrated built-in attitude with the aid of view built-in demand built integrated and setbacks as possibilities for built-in integrated and growth. recognize that failure and adversity are herbal components of the human level built integrated and that resilience is built via built integrated and overcome integrated obstacles. attention on development built-in integrated perfection and rejoicing small victories along the way.

Commit Built-in to Self-mirrored image and built-in:

Commit to ongo built-in self-mirrored image and built-increase integrated as you figure to venture poor thoughts integrated and beliefs. Set apart time for integrated introspection, journal built-in, and self-evaluation to song your development and discover regions for further development. celebrate your

Successes and acknowledge the courage and resilience it takes to undertake built integrated deeply integrated rebuilt-and patterns of built-in.
With the aid of built-in and difficult negative built

Integrated and ideals, integrated can domesticate extra emotional resilience, self-compassion, and nicely-built-in. Through focus, self-reflection, and a dedication to built-in, it's far possible to transform negative thought styles and cultivate a more high quality and empowered built-indset.

Chapter 5:

2) Cultivating a nice attitude through Affirmations and Gratitude

Cultivating a first rate thoughts-set is important for promoting highbrow and emotional well-being, resilience, and ordinary existence pleasure. Affirmations and gratitude practices are effective devices that could assist humans shift their mind-set, foster optimism, and domesticate a deeper experience of gratitude and appreciation for life's benefits. With the aid of incorporating affirmations and gratitude into each day's physical activities, humans can educate their minds to consciousness on the factors of lifestyles and conquer bad notion patterns.

Know-how Affirmations:
Affirmations are nice statements or terms that are repeated often to verify and improve preferred ideals, attitudes, and behaviours. Affirmations are designed to assignment terrible self-communicate, boost, and domesticate a experience of empowerment and Examples of affirmations embody statements consisting of "i am worth of love and admire," "I agree with in my abilities to gain my desires," and "i'm deserving of happiness and success."

Training Affirmations frequently:
Encompass affirmations into your day by day habitual via setting apart committed time each day to copy affirmations aloud or silently.

select affirmations that resonate with you for my part and reflect regions of your life where you would love to enjoy effective change or increase. Repeat affirmations with conviction and aim, focusing on the meaning and emotion in the back of each declaration.

Specialising in the present and future:

Affirmations are handiest while targeted on the prevailing second and framed inside the fantastic gift traumatic. In preference to stating what you need to trade or advantage inside the future, affirmations affirm the reality of your goals and aspirations as if they may be already right. This enables shift your attitude from taken into consideration one among lack and difficulty to taken into consideration one in every abundance and possibility.

Difficult terrible idea styles:

Affirmations serve as powerful system for tough terrible belief styles and ideals. by means of the use of consciously replacing horrible self-speak with high-high excellent affirmations, humans can reprogram their subconscious minds and domesticate a greater optimistic and empowered attitude

Affirmations assist counteract emotions of self-doubt, worry, and inadequacy by way of instilling self belief, self-compassion, and resilience.

Practising Gratitude:

Gratitude is the workout of intentionally focusing on the additives of lifestyles and expressing appreciation for the benefits, massive and small, that surround us.

Gratitude promotes a shift in angle from scarcity to abundance and cultivates a deeper enjoyment of contentment, joy, and success. Gratitude practices may additionally encompass keeping a gratitude journal, expressing gratitude to others, and taking time to have a laugh with and appreciate existence's clean pleasures.

Maintaining a Gratitude magazine:

Preserve a gratitude magazine to record every day reflections at the matters, people, and studies you're grateful for. Set aside time each day to mirror on 3 to 5 assets you are thankful for and write them right down to your magazine. domesticate a mindset of appreciation and mindfulness as you acknowledge and rejoice the abundance and splendour in your lifestyles.

Savouring Moments of joy and Connection:

Take time to get delight from and absolutely revel in moments of joy, splendour, and connection to your lifestyles. Pause to recognize the points of hobby, sounds, and sensations of the prevailing second, whether or not or no longer it is a stunning sunset, a heartfelt communique with a cherished one, or a simple act of kindness. cultivate mindfulness and presence as you immerse yourself completely in these moments of gratitude and appreciation.

Expressing Gratitude to Others:

Specific gratitude to others for his or her kindness, aid, and contributions to your existence. Take time to renowned and thank pals, circle of relatives, participants, colleagues, and mentors for their generosity, encouragement, and first-class impact. Expressing gratitude fosters deeper connections and strengthens relationships even as spreading positivity and kindness to others.

Cultivating an mindset of Abundance:
Domesticate an mind-set of abundance with the aid of that specialise in what you've got in preference to what you lack. Shift your mind-set from one among scarcity and trouble to take into consideration one in every abundance and opportunity. recognize the abundance of benefits and possibilities that surround you, and method existence with an open coronary heart and a spirit of gratitude and appreciation.

Integrating Affirmations and Gratitude into each day existence:
Integrate affirmations and gratitude practices into your daily lifestyles to domesticate a mind-set and enhance regular proper-being. begin every day with affirmations that encourage and uplift you, and end each day with reflections at the stuff you are grateful for. Infuse your interactions, sports, and reviews with positivity, optimism, and appreciation, and watch as your attitude and outlook on life remodel for the higher.

With the resource of cultivating a positive mind-set through affirmations and gratitude, individuals can nurture a deeper enjoyment of self-popularity, resilience, and happiness. Through constant workout and aware cognizance, affirmations and gratitude become effective equipment for remodelling poor idea patterns, embracing life's advantages, and developing a greater gratifying and substantial existence.

Chapter 5:
3) Techniques for Overcoming Self-Doubt and Boosting Self-confidence.

Self-doubt can be a outstanding barrier to boom, fulfilment. Overcoming self-doubt and boosting self-self belief are crucial for understanding one's full capability, pursuing goals with courage and backbone, and navigating lifestyles's worrying conditions with resilience and optimism. Fortunately, there are numerous strategies and techniques that humans can hire to overcome self-doubt and cultivate more self-confidence.

Choose out and task terrible Self-talk:

Terrible self-talk is a not unusual contributor to self-doubt. start via identifying and tough a bad mind and ideals about yourself. be privy to your internal speak and word while self-doubt arises. mission terrible mind through asking yourself if they'll be based totally on statistics or distorted perceptions. update awful self-speak with exquisite affirmations and empowering ideals approximately your abilities and self self-esteem.

Set sensible dreams and expectancies:

Setting realistic dreams and expectancies can help build self notion by presenting a clean roadmap for success. ruin larger dreams down into smaller, possible responsibilities, and feature a laugh at your improvement alongside the way. Setbacks and disasters are inevitable components of the adventure, however they offer precious possibilities for gaining knowledge of and boom. embody demanding situations as opportunities to stretch your talents and grow in your comfort area.

Interest in Strengths and Achievements:

Shift your focus from perceived weaknesses for your strengths and past achievements. replicate in your accomplishments, competencies, and excessive great traits, and renowned the development you have made. maintain a magazine or gratitude listing in which you could file your successes, regardless of how small. Celebrating your strengths and achievements reinforces an awesome self-picture and boosts self-self warranty.

Exercise Self-Compassion and reputation:

Domesticate self-compassion and recognition through treating yourself with kindness, understanding, and empathy. take into account that self-doubt is a herbal part of human enjoyment and that everyone remembers moments of insecurity and vulnerability. exercising self-care sports activities which include meditation, mindfulness, and self-care to nurture your emotional proper-being and sell self-recognition.

Are searching for assistance and feedback:

Attain out to rely on friends, family people, mentors, or experts for assistance and remarks. surround yourself with powerful impacts who consider your capacity and inspire you to pursue your goals. are attempting to find optimistic remarks from others to benefit perception into your strengths and regions for improvement. receive remarks with an open mind and use it as an opportunity for growth and development.

Take movement and include challenges:

Take motion notwithstanding self-doubt and worry of failure. embody disturbing conditions as opportunities to look at, broaden, and expand your abilities. Step outside of your consolation place and take calculated dangers that push you beyond your perceived limits. Every small victory and accomplishment builds self assurance and reinforces your perception in yourself.

Exercise Visualization and Imagery:

Use visualisation and superb imagery to imagine yourself succeeding and reaching your goals. Create mental pics of yourself overcoming barriers, getting to know new abilities, and carrying out your goals. Visualise achievement in first rate detail, engaging all your senses, and immerse yourself inside the enjoyment of achieving your goals. Visualisation primes your mind for achievement and builds self notion in your capacity to show your goals into reality.

Develop Competence via learning and boom:

Put money into your non-public private and expert improvement through continuously mastering and developing. collect new know-how, skills, and abilities which might be relevant to your dreams and aspirations. Take non private, attend workshops, and are trying to find out opportunities for mentorship and skills-constructing. growing competence enhances self-self assurance and empowers you to tackle stressful conditions with greater skills and information.

Exercise Assertiveness and Self-Advocacy:

Exercising assertiveness and self-advocacy through using expressing your dreams, critiques, and obstacles with self guarantee and readability. learn how to assert yourself in a deferential and assertive way, even in tough or uncomfortable conditions. Set limitations that shield your well-being and honour your values, and assertively speak your expectancies to others.

Have a good time development and embrace Imperfection:

Have fun with your progress and accomplishments, irrespective of how small. well known your efforts and achievements, and supply your self credit rating for the stairs you have taken toward your desires. encompass imperfection as a natural part of the human revel in and recognize that growth and improvement are nonlinear procedures. deal with setbacks and screw ups as opportunities for analysing and resilience-constructing, instead of motives to doubt yourself.

By means of imposing those techniques for overcoming self-doubt and boosting self-self perception, people can domesticate a more exceptional and empowered mindset that allows them to pursue their desires and aspirations with courage, resilience, and unwavering self-perception. take into account that self-self assurance is an ability that may be developed and reinforced through the years through steady exercise, self-reflected photography, and a willingness to embrace challenges and possibilities for boom.

Chapter 6:

Time thinking in movement: Case research and Examples:-

1) Real-lifestyles stories of people who've converted Their houses and Minds the use of Time thinking

In the adventure toward developing harmonious homes and non violent minds, the concept of Time thinking has emerged as a transformative tool for plenty of individuals. Through the lens of real-life tales, we witness the profound impact that point wandering has had on remodelling each bodily living areas and intellectual landscapes, mainly to more readability, productiveness, and emotional proper-being.

Sarah's story:
From Chaos to Calm

Sarah, a busy expert and mom of , determined herself crushed by way of the regular needs of work, own family, and household responsibilities. Her domestic life became cluttered, disorganised, and chaotic, mirroring the turmoil she felt within. struggling to stabilise her commitments and keep a sense of peace, Sarah turned to Time thinking for guidance.

Through intentional time management and prioritisation strategies, Sarah learned to allocate her time and electricity correctly, that specialise in what absolutely mattered most to her and her own family. via enforcing daily routines, scheduling dedicated decluttering sessions, and placing barriers around her time, Sarah step by step transformed her domestic right into a sanctuary of order and tranquillity.

As her outside surroundings became extra streamlined and potential, Sarah observed a profound shift in her mental country. She skillfully multiplied readability, cognizance, and a feel of empowerment as she regained control over her time and area. With a newfound experience of stability and reason, Sarah changed into capable of navigating lifestyles's challenges with greater resilience and inner peace.

David's journey:
 Overcoming crush

David, a recent college graduate embarking on his career journey, discovered himself beaten by way of the transition to maturity and the pressures of setting up himself within the professional world. His tiny rental served as a steady reminder of his struggles, cluttered with property and without proposal.

Feeling trapped in a cycle of procrastination and self-doubt, David turned to Time thinking as a catalyst for exchange. He embraced the ideas of prioritisation, awareness, and intentional movement, making use of them to each his personal and expert pursuits. via placing clear goals, breaking them down into viable tasks, and allocating his time strategically, David started to make meaningful progress toward his aspirations.

As he simplified his dwelling space, decluttered his mind, and embraced a greater aware approach to time management, David experienced a profound transformation. He created a renewed sense of motive, self assurance, and self-perception, unlocking his full capacity and paving the manner for private and expert increase.

Maria's course to Peace:
Embracing Mindfulness and Gratitude

Maria, a committed homemaker and caregiver, determined herself feeling overwhelmed and depleted through the needs of her role. Juggling household chores, circle of relatives responsibilities, and caregiving duties left her feeling tired and disconnected from herself. In search of solace amidst the chaos, Maria turned to Time questioning as a supply of concept and guidance.

Through the workout of mindfulness, gratitude, and intentional dwelling, Maria embarked on a journey of self-discovery and internal transformation. She was created to cultivate a deeper awareness of the existing 2nd, savouring existence's clean pleasures and finding splendour within the everyday. with the aid of expressing gratitude for the blessings in her existence and embracing an mind-set of abundance, Maria cultivated a profound sense of contentment and fulfilment.

As she infused her every day sporting events with mindfulness practices, Maria observed a profound shift in her attitude and well-being. She felt extra gift, grounded, and related to herself and those around her. By means of prioritising self-care, putting obstacles, and embracing moments of stillness and mirrored image, Maria created a home environment that radiated warmth, love, and calmness.

Those real-life tales function as powerful reminders of the transformative electricity of Time questioning in reshaping both our external environments and inner landscapes. Through intentional time control, prioritisation, and mindfulness practices, people can create homes and minds that mirror their values, aspirations, and inner most desires. As we embody the principles of Time questioning in our personal lives, we unencumbered the ability for profound non-public growth, achievement, and lasting happiness.

Chapter 6:

2) Making use of Time questioning ideas to different residing conditions and challenges

Time wandering concepts provide a versatile framework that may be applied to diverse living conditions and challenges, empowering individuals to manipulate their time, area, and attitude more efficiently. Whether navigating busy schedules, adjusting to lifestyles transitions, or searching for more balance and success, the standards of Time thinking offer practical steerage and techniques for optimising each day exercises and fostering non-public increase.

Navigating Busy existence:

For people with disturbing schedules and multiple obligations, Time thinking offers precious tools for prioritisation, time management, and stress reduction. By figuring out key priorities and allocating time and energy consequently, busy professionals, parents, and caregivers can streamline their routines, reduce distractions, and become aware of activities that align with their desires and values. Time-blocking off strategies, task prioritisation, and delegation strategies enable individuals to maximise productivity and create area for rest, rest, and self-care amidst the hustle and bustle of daily life.

Managing Transitions and life modifications:

Life transitions, which include beginning a brand new process, transferring to a new city, or adjusting to parenthood, frequently come with specific challenges and uncertainties. Time thinking standards provide a roadmap for navigating transitions with readability, resilience, and adaptability. by embracing flexibility, putting practical expectancies, and practising self-compassion, people can navigate durations of trade with more ease and confidence. Time wandering encourages individuals to be conscious of the existing moment, agree with their capability to evolve and grow, and embrace new possibilities for getting to know and personal improvement.

Creating Harmonious dwelling Environments:

Whether or not dwelling in a small rental, a suburban home, or a shared residing area, Time thinking principles can assist people create harmonious environments that sell productiveness, creativity, and nicely-being. by decluttering bodily spaces, organising assets, and optimising furniture preparations, people can maximise the functionality and aesthetics of their living environments. Time questioning also emphasises the significance of creating barriers, fostering open communication, and cultivating a feel of network and belonging within shared dwelling areas.

Balancing paintings and private existence:

Accomplishing a healthful work-life balance is a not unusual venture in a trendy fast-paced world. Time thinking encourages people to establish clear limitations between paintings and private lifestyles, prioritise self-care and amusement sports, and cultivate meaningful connections with cherished ones. by placing sensible expectancies, handling time successfully, and honouring non-public values and priorities, people can create a sense of equilibrium and success in each expert and personal spheres.

Cultivating Mindfulness and nicely-Being:

Time thinking principles emphasise the importance of mindfulness, self-recognition, and holistic well-being in all aspects of life. By practising mindfulness techniques including meditation, deep respiration, and aware living, people can cultivate an extra sense of presence, calmness, and internal peace. Time wandering encourages individuals to prioritise activities that nourish the thoughts, frame, and spirit, which includes exercise, nature walks, creative expression, and first-rate time spent with cherished ones.

Placing and reaching non-public desires:

Whether pursuing career aspirations, private development targets, or health and health dreams, Time Wandering gives a framework for placing sensible desires, breaking them down into actionable steps, and tracking progress over time. By adopting a boom attitude, embracing demanding situations, and celebrating small victories, people can stay inspired and resilient within the pursuit of their dreams. Time questioning encourages individuals to consciousness on non-stop development, adaptability, and lifelong mastering as they strive to gain their full ability.

In precise, applying Time thinking concepts to special dwelling situations and challenges empowers individuals to manipulate their time, area, and mind-set so one can lead greater balanced, pleasant, and cause-pushed lives. With the aid of embracing flexibility, prioritisation, and self-attention, individuals can navigate lifestyles's complexities with self belief, resilience, and an experience of reason. As we combine Time thinking concepts into our day by day routines and selection-making procedures, we liberate the potential for private boom, success, and lasting happiness in all areas of our lives.

Chapter 7:

Nurturing Sustainable conduct for lengthy-term fulfilment:-

1) Organising exercises and systems to preserve a Balanced domestic and thoughts

Organising workouts and systems is crucial for maintaining a balanced and harmonious domestic environment at the same time as nurturing a peaceful and resilient attitude. By means of enforcing based workouts and effective structures, individuals can streamline each day's duties, reduce strain, and create a sense of stability and order in both their bodily surroundings and mental well-being.

Developing Morning and nighttime routines:

Morning and night routines serve as anchor factors within the day, assisting individuals start and cease each day on a fine note. Morning routines may additionally encompass sports which include meditation, exercising, journaling, and enjoying a nutritious breakfast to set a positive tone for the day ahead. evening exercises may also involve winding down with rest techniques, reflecting at the day's activities, and getting ready for restful sleep.

Setting clean each day Priorities:

Prioritisation is key to retaining stability and cognizance amidst the demands of each day life. via setting clean priorities and identifying the most important tasks for every day, individuals can allocate their time and strength successfully. utilising time-blockading techniques and to-do lists helps people live prepared and centred on obligations that align with their desires and values.

Imposing household structures:

Household systems are important for managing daily chores and obligations correctly. enforcing structures for meal planning, grocery purchasing, cleaning, and company helps streamline household duties and decreases selection fatigue. By setting up exact instances for particular sports and delegating duties amongst household members, individuals can create an experience of shared duty and cooperation inside the home.

Practising mindful Time management:

Mindful time management entails being gifted and intentional with how time is spent. via identifying time wasters and distractions, people can reclaim valuable time for sports that make a contribution to their proper-being and personal growth. placing boundaries round era use, scheduling ordinary breaks, and practising focused interest strategies decorate productivity and reduce emotions of crush.

Embracing Flexibility and adaptableness:

Whilst workouts and structures provide structure and predictability, it's critical to remain flexible and adaptable to exchange. existence is full of surprising occasions and demanding situations that may disrupt hooked up exercises. Embracing a mind-set of flexibility and adaptability permits people to adjust their workouts and structures as wanted, without turning into beaten or discouraged.

Incorporating Self-Care Practices:

Self-care is an important issue of keeping balance and well-being. Incorporating self-care practices into each day exercises guarantees that individuals prioritise their physical, emotional, and mental health. activities inclusive of exercising, relaxation strategies, hobbies, and spending time in nature refill strength reserves and promote universal resilience and vitality.

Fostering Open communique:

Effective conversation is vital for keeping concord and cohesion in the domestic. Normal family conferences provide an opportunity for open speaking, problem-solving, and purpose-putting. Encouraging every member of the family to express their wishes, worries, and ideas fosters a feeling of mutual admiration and understanding, strengthening family bonds and promoting a supportive and nurturing environment.

Reflecting and Adjusting as wished:

A regular mirrored image allows individuals to assess the effectiveness in their exercises and systems and make modifications as wanted. Taking time to assess what's operating well and what can be stepped forward allows people to refine their approach and optimise their routines for extra performance and delight. Embracing a boom mind-set and viewing challenges as possibilities for gaining knowledge of and boom fosters non-stop improvement and version.

By setting up routines and systems to preserve a balanced home and mind, individuals can create a supportive and nurturing environment that promotes proper-being, productiveness, and resilience. Through intentional planning, effective communique, and a commitment to self-care, individuals cultivate an experience of balance and harmony that complements their quality of existence and strengthens their connections with others. As they prioritise their physical and emotional needs, individuals lay the inspiration for a satisfying and meaningful life characterised by way of stability, cause, and pleasure.

Chapter 7:

2) Integrating Time wondering Into Your everyday lifestyles for Lasting results

Time wandering gives a transformative technique to coping with time, space, and mindset, empowering people to steer more intentional, balanced, and fulfilling lives. By integrating Time thinking ideas into their everyday routines and decision-making procedures, individuals can cultivate more readability, productivity, and proper-being that lead to lasting consequences and private boom.

Knowledge Time questioning ideas:

Time wondering includes a mind-set shift that prioritises intentionality, cognizance, and mindfulness in how time is controlled and utilised. Principal to Time wandering are standards which include prioritisation, aim-putting, and mindful cognizance of ways time is spent. via information these principles, people can begin to harness the electricity of Time questioning to create positive changes in their lives.

Setting clean Intentions and goals:

Integrating Time questioning starts with putting clean intentions and desires for a way time may be allocated and priorities may be controlled. people are encouraged to perceive their centre values, aspirations, and regions of attention, and to align their day by day activities and commitments therefore. By way of organising significant desires and milestones, individuals create a roadmap for attaining lasting consequences and personal achievement.

Practising Time management techniques:

Time control techniques are important equipment for imposing Time thinking principles into everyday lifestyles. techniques inclusive of time-blockading, task prioritisation, and setting cut-off dates help individuals manage their time greater effectively and pay attention to activities that align with their goals and priorities. By allocating time deliberately and keeping off distractions, people maximise productivity and gain extra balance and pride.

Embracing aware focus and Presence:

Mindful attention is a cornerstone of Time thinking, encouraging individuals to be fully gifted and engaged in every moment. By means of training mindfulness strategies inclusive of deep breathing, meditation, and conscious residing, people cultivate a deeper sense of focus and connection to the prevailing moment. Mindfulness enables individuals to live grounded, reduce stress, and make intentional alternatives that support their proper-being and private increase.

Growing Sustainable conduct and routines:

Integrating Time wandering into daily life involves creating sustainable behaviour and workouts that guide lengthy-term success and proper-being. People are endorsed to establish regular every day exercises, rituals, and systems that sell productiveness, creativity, and stability. by incorporating self-care practices, normal exercising, and downtime into their schedules, individuals nurture their bodily, emotional, and mental health.

Reflecting and Adjusting as needed:

Reflection is a crucial issue of integrating Time wandering into everyday lifestyles, permitting individuals to evaluate their progress, pick out regions for improvement, and make changes as wished. an ordinary self-mirrored image prompts people to evaluate how effectively they are dealing with their time, strength, and assets, and to direction-accurate as necessary. Embracing a growth attitude and viewing challenges as possibilities for learning and growth fosters resilience and adaptability.

Celebrating development and Milestones:

Celebrating progress and milestones is a crucial part of integrating Time thinking into everyday life. By acknowledging achievements, large and small, individuals improve advantageous behaviour and behaviours and stay stimulated to preserve their adventure of private growth and development. Celebrating progress fosters a sense of accomplishment and gratitude, fueling momentum and inspiring continued effort and willpower.

Fostering responsibility and support:

Fostering duty and guidance is prime to sustaining the practice of Time wondering over the long term. individuals can seek accountability companions, join supportive groups, or enlist the help of a train or mentor to offer encouragement, steerage, and accountability. By surrounding themselves with like-minded those who percentages their dedication to boom and development, people stay encouraged and inspired to combine Time thinking into their day by day lives.

Through integrating Time thinking into their daily lives, people release the capacity for lasting outcomes, private achievement, and meaningful trade. via intentional time management, mindful focus, and intention-oriented movement, people create an existence characterised with the aid of purpose, stability, and joy. As they embody the principles of Time questioning and commit to ongoing increase and reflection, people cultivate the abilities and mind-set had to thrive in an ever-changing international.

Chapter 7:

3) Hints for Overcoming Setbacks and Staying inspired

Setbacks are an inevitable part of existence's adventure, but how we respond to them could make all of the difference in our capability to acquire our desires and live influenced. Whether or not going through demanding situations in our private or professional lives, studying to conquer setbacks is critical for retaining resilience, perseverance, and an advantageous attitude. right here are a few recommendations

For overcoming setbacks and staying encouraged:

Renowned Your feelings: it's important to know and validate your feelings while confronted with setbacks. allow yourself to revel in emotions which include frustration, sadness, or disappointment. Denying or suppressing your emotions can result in multiplied pressure and tension. keep in mind that setbacks are a regular part of the adventure toward fulfilment and increase.

Practice Self-Compassion:

Be kind to yourself at some point of tough instances. deal with yourself with the identical compassion and know-how that you could provide to a chum handling comparable demanding situations. Keep in mind that setbacks no longer define your real worth or abilities. exercise self-care sports which includes meditation, workout, or spending time with loved ones to nurture your emotional properly-being.

Reframe Your attitude:

In place of viewing setbacks as failures, reframe them as possibilities for getting to know and increase. reflect on what you may study from the entertainment and the way it assists you to end up stronger and additional resilient within the future. Adopting a boom mind-set allows you to technique setbacks with interest and optimism, as opposed to defeat. Through the workout of mindfulness, gratitude, and intentional dwelling, Maria embarked on a journey of self-discovery and internal transformation. She was created to cultivate a deeper awareness of the existing 2nd, savouring existence's clean pleasures and finding splendour within the everyday. With the aid of expressing gratitude for the blessings in her life and embracing a mind-set of abundance, Maria cultivated a profound experience of contentment and fulfilment. As she infused her daily sporting events with mindfulness practices, Maria observed a profound shift in her angle and nicely-being.

Damage It Down:

While confronted with a setback, wreck down the trouble into smaller, greater achievable additives. cognizance of taking small, actionable steps in the direction of addressing the difficulty in preference to turning into crushed by the significance of the setback. by breaking down the trouble into smaller obligations, you can hold a feel of development and momentum.

Seek assist:

Reach out to pals, family participants, mentors, or colleagues for help and encouragement at some point of hard instances. Sharing your stories with others can offer perspective, validation, and emotional aid. surround yourself with fantastic people who trust in your talents and provide positive comments and steering.

Live flexible and Adapt:

Be open to adapting your desires and plans in response to setbacks. Once in a while, setbacks present sudden opportunities or opportunity pathways toward achieving your objectives. stay flexible and inclined to discover new processes or views. embody the uncertainty and accept it as true within your capacity to navigate challenges with resilience and creativity.

Rejoice progress, no longer Perfection:

Rejoice your development and achievements, regardless of how small. apprehend and rejoice the efforts you've made toward your dreams, even supposing you have not yet performed the favoured final results. Celebrating progress reinforces tremendous behaviours and motivates you to preserve moving ahead, even within the face of setbacks.

Recognition on What you could control:

When setbacks occur, cognizance on what you may control rather than living on elements outside of you have an impact on. become aware of actionable steps and areas where you may exert an impact on and take proactive measures to deal with them. by specialising in what you could manage, you regain an experience of organisation and empowerment over your occasions.

Visualise fulfilment:

Visualise yourself overcoming limitations and attaining your goals. Create intellectual pictures of achievement and envision yourself navigating demanding situations with self belief and backbone. Visualisation techniques can help boost motivation, decorate attention, and enhance an effective attitude, even during challenging instances.

Preserve angle:

Keep setbacks in angle and avoid catastrophizing or magnifying their importance. remember the fact that setbacks are transient and do now not define your closing capacity or well worth. keep an extended-term angle and consciousness on the bigger image of your goals and aspirations. believe in your potential to overcome limitations and stay devoted in your journey of increase and self-discovery.

by implementing those recommendations for overcoming setbacks and staying stimulated, you could navigate demanding situations with resilience, optimism, and style. include setbacks as opportunities for increase, learning, and self-discovery, and use them to propel yourself ahead on the course closer to reaching your desires and aspirations. With willpower, perseverance, and a superb mind-set, you could overcome any setback and emerge more potent, wiser, and extra resilient than ever earlier than.

Chapter 8:

Embracing a existence of harmony and properly-being:-

1) Reflecting to your journey toward mental and domestic clarity

A mirrored image is a powerful tool for gaining perception, information, and attitude on our reports, picks, and increase. When it comes to achieving mental and domestic clarity, taking time to reflect on our journey is vital for deepening self-awareness, figuring out styles, and charting our route closer to greater harmony and balance. here is a complete description of the technique of reflecting for your journey towards

Intellectual and home clarity:

Growing area for mirrored image:

Start by creating a quiet and secure space

Wherein you could engage in reflective exercise without distractions.

Set aside committed time for a mirrored image, whether it's a few minutes each day or an extended period on a weekly or foundation. Disconnecting from virtual devices and external stimuli month-to-month foster a feel of internal calm and consciousness.

Reviewing Your development:

Take stock of your journey in the direction of intellectual and home readability by reviewing your progress and accomplishments. reflect at the modifications you've made, demanding situations you've triumphed over, and milestones you've reached alongside the manner. rejoice your successes and well know the boom and transformation you have skilled, regardless of how small or incremental.

Exploring Your challenges and Setbacks:

Delve into the demanding situations and setbacks you've encountered to your adventure in the direction of intellectual and domestic readability. mirror the classes discovered from those stories and keep in mind how they have formed your increase and resilience. perceive any ordinary patterns or limitations that may be hindering your development and discover techniques for overcoming them in the future.

Examining Your Values and Priorities:

Reflect on your values, priorities, and aspirations in each of your intellectual and home lifestyles. don't forget whether or not your current life-style aligns together with your centre values and whether or not your property surroundings displays your priorities and dreams. explore areas in which you could need to realign your actions and alternatives with your deepest values and intentions.

Working towards Gratitude and Appreciation:

Cultivate a sense of gratitude and appreciation for the blessings and possibilities that have enriched your journey towards intellectual and home clarity. reflect on the people, studies, and assets which have supported and stimulated you alongside the way. specific gratitude for the increase, insights, and moments of readability that have illuminated your direction.

Figuring out areas for increase and improvement:

An honest mirrored image includes figuring out areas where you can keep growing and improving in each of your mental and domestic life. remember regions where you will be experiencing resistance, stagnation, or unfulfilled capability. discover possibilities for personal development, skill-constructing, and self-care that align along with your dreams and aspirations.

Setting Intentions for the future:

Use a mirrored image as a springboard for putting intentions and goals for destiny. clarify your vision for intellectual and domestic clarity and articulate particular moves and steps you could take to appear this imaginative and prescient. Set sensible and viable dreams that resonate with your values and priorities, and commit to taking steady action toward their attainment.

Working towards Mindfulness and Presence:

Infuse your reflective practice with mindfulness and presence by anchoring yourself inside the gift second. be aware of thoughts, feelings, and sensations as they arise without judgement or attachment. cultivate a feel of curiosity and openness as you explore your internal panorama and the dynamics of your house environment.

Searching for help and accountability:

Engage in reflective dialogue with relied on buddies, circle of relatives, individuals, mentors, or coaches who can provide aid, guidance, and duty to your adventure toward mental and domestic readability. share your reflections openly and listen with an open coronary heart to the views and insights of others. include the electricity of network and connection in fostering growth and transformation.

Committing to Ongoing mirrored image and increase:

A mirrored image isn't always a one-time occasion however an ongoing practice that evolves over time. decide to integrate reflection into your everyday existence as a supply of insight, proposal, and renewal. embrace the journey in the direction of intellectual and home clarity as a technique of non-stop getting to know, model, and self-discovery, and accept as true within your innate capacity to navigate existence's complexities with know-how and beauty.

By conducting reflective exercise, you deepen your information of yourself and your environment, domesticate extra readability and perception, and align your movements together with your innermost values and intentions. embody reflection as a sacred ritual that nourishes your soul and illuminates your direction towards intellectual and domestic readability, one second of introspection at a time.

Chapter 8:

2) Celebrating Achievements and increase alongside the manner

Celebrating achievements and growth alongside the journey is an essential issue of personal development and self-care. It is an exercise that acknowledges progress, fosters motivation, and cultivates a feel of success and gratitude. here's a full description of the importance and benefits of celebrating achievements and increase along the way:

Reputation of development:

Celebrating achievements serves as a reputation of the progress we have made on our adventure. it is a possibility to renowned the attempt, willpower, and perseverance we've invested in pursuing our goals and aspirations. via pausing to have fun milestones, each huge and small, we verify our dedication to personal boom and improvement.

Boosting Motivation and self assurance:

Celebrating achievements boosts motivation and confidence, presenting a feel of validation and encouragement to keep shifting ahead. when we understand our accomplishments, we make stronger high quality behaviours and beliefs about our competencies. This renewed experience of self assurance fuels our momentum and empowers us to address new demanding situations with courage and exuberance.

Cultivating a tremendous mindset:

Celebrating achievements cultivates a superb attitude via focusing our attention on what we've been given and performed in preference to what we've got yet to acquire. It shifts our mind-set from shortage to abundance, fostering gratitude and appreciation for the improvement we've made.

attitude allows us to approach demanding situations with optimism and resilience, knowing that we have the potential to overcome boundaries and thrive.

Fostering a lifestyle of celebration:

Cultivating a lifestyle of celebration within our non-public and professional lives creates an environment in which achievements are valued and recognized. by sharing our successes with others, we encourage and uplift those around us, fostering a feel of camaraderie and aid. Celebrating achievements together strengthens relationships and builds a feel of a network based totally on mutual encouragement and admiration.

Reflecting on boom and getting to know:

Celebrating achievements gives an opportunity for a mirrored image on our increase and learning studies. It lets us pause and well know the instructions we've found out, the limitations we have conquered, and the insights we've received along the way. Reflecting on our adventure allows us to gain an angle and respect the depth of our private transformation and improvement.

Sustaining Momentum and development:

Celebrating achievements sustains momentum and progress via acknowledging the incremental steps we take towards our dreams. It fuels our motivation to strive for excellence and excellence and reminds us of the significance of perseverance and resilience inside the face of adversity. via celebrating achievements, we reinforce our dedication to private and expert boom, making sure that we live targeted and driven in our direction.

Honouring and price:

Celebrating achievements honours our and fee as individuals. It affirms our inherent self confidence and validates our contributions and accomplishments. Recognizing our achievements reminds us that we're capable, deserving, and worthy of fulfilment and fulfilment. It instils an experience of pleasure and self-admire that empowers us to pursue our dreams and aspirations with integrity and motive.

Growing Lasting recollections and Traditions:

Celebrating achievements creates lasting memories and traditions that enhance our lives and create bonds with the ones we cherish. Whether or not through unique rituals, ceremonies, or easy acts of acknowledgment, celebrations mark enormous milestones and create significant connections with others. These shared reviews beef up our relationships and create an experience of belonging and belonging and camaraderie.

In conclusion,
 Celebrating achievements and boom along the way is a powerful exercise that nourishes the soul, uplifts the spirit, and fuels the journey in the direction of non-public and professional achievement. By embracing the attitude of a birthday party, we honour our development, cultivate resilience, and encourage others to attain their complete capacity. Let us rejoice each breakthrough with gratitude, joy, and a deep appreciation for the richness of human enjoyment.

Chapter 8:

3) Embracing a lifestyle of stability, Peace, and achievement

Embracing a life-style of stability, peace, and fulfilment is a deliberate desire to live with intention and motive, looking for harmony and contentment in every issue of existence. It entails nurturing the thoughts, body, and spirit while cultivating a sense of internal tranquillity and satisfaction. here's a complete description of what it way to embody this kind of way of life:

1. Locating balance Amidst lifestyles's demands:

A way of life of balance acknowledges the importance of allocating time and energy to various sides of lifestyles, such as work, relationships, private increase, and amusement. It entails placing obstacles and priorities to make certain that no unmarried factor dominates our attention at the fee of others. By striving for equilibrium, we create an area for fulfilment and well-being to flourish in all regions of life.

2. Cultivating inner Peace and Serenity:

Internal peace is the cornerstone of a balanced lifestyle, emanating from a nation of calmness and recognition within oneself. Embracing a life-style of peace includes practices such as meditation, .

mindfulness, and self-reflection, which assist quiet the mind and foster a deep experience of tranquillity. Through mindfulness, we learn how to permit a cross of issues, regrets, and anxieties, embracing each second with grace and presence

3. Searching for fulfilment in meaningful hobbies:

Achievement arises from accomplishing activities and hobbies that resonate with our values, passions, and experience of cause. It involves aligning our actions with our deepest aspirations and contributing to causes more than ourselves. Whether or not through innovative expression, personal increase endeavours, or acts of service, we find fulfilment in moments of connection, contribution, and self-expression.

4. Nurturing wholesome Relationships and Connections:

Meaningful relationships are essential to a satisfying life, offering love, aid, and companionship alongside the adventure. Embracing a life-style of balance and fulfilment entails nurturing real connections with others based on acceptance as true with, empathy, and mutual respect. through fostering healthy communique, emotional intimacy, and shared stories, we increase our lives and deepen our experience of belonging and connection.

5. Residing Mindfully and presently:

Mindfulness is the exercise of being absolutely present and engaged in every second, unfastened from judgement or distraction. Embracing a lifestyle of stability and fulfilment includes cultivating mindfulness in regular activities, from eating and on foot to working and speaking. by grounding ourselves in the gift moment, we cultivate a deeper appreciation for existence's easy pleasures and increase resilience within the face of demanding situations.

6. Self-care is an important difficulty of a balanced and pleasant lifestyle, encompassing practices that nourish and rejuvenate the mind, frame, and spirit. It includes prioritising rest, relaxation, and sports activities that promote physical fitness, emotional nicely-being, and non secular renewal. via honouring our needs and barriers, we domesticate resilience, strength, and a deeper sense of self-cognizance and compassion.

7. Schooling Gratitude and Appreciation"

Refers to the exercise of actively cultivating a mind-set of thankfulness and recognition within a training or academic context. It entails acknowledging and expressing appreciation for the opportunities, assets, and help acquired for the duration of the schooling method.

This concept entails greater than just pronouncing "thank you." It includes deepening one's attention to the fee derived from training stories, mentors, friends, and the studying surroundings. Through consciously focusing on gratitude and appreciation, people can decorate their mastering journey, foster effective relationships, and expand an attitude that promotes boom and resilience.

In realistic phrases, schooling gratitude and appreciation can also involve sports consisting of maintaining a gratitude journal, reflecting on specific components of education that one is grateful for, expressing gratitude to trainers and associates, and actively seeking opportunities to reveal appreciation inside the schooling network.

Typically, education gratitude and appreciation serve as effective equipment for reinforcing personal and professional development, fostering a high-quality gaining knowledge of surroundings, and nurturing significant connections in the schooling context.

8. Embracing growth and Evolution:

Increase and evolution are inherent aspects of the human revel in, inviting us to embody exchange and transformation with openness and hobby. Embracing a way of life of balance and achievement includes welcoming possibilities for getting to know, self-discovery, and private boom. With the resource of embracing our strengths and worrying conditions, we extend our horizons, deepen our know-how, and unleash our complete capacity.

In essence, embracing a manner of existence of stability, peace, and achievement is an adventure of self-discovery, self-care, and self-reputation. It consists of aligning our movements with our values, fostering significant connections, and locating contentment in the present 2d. by way of the use of nurturing inner peace, cultivating gratitude, and embracing increase, we create lives which may be wealthy, sizeable, and deeply enjoyable, honouring the splendour and sacredness of the human experience.

Finally, Summary this book :-

"Winning time & think manage: manage your private home without Decluttering Your thoughts" gives a clean method to dealing with your private home and mental well-being without the strain of conventional decluttering methods. This insightful guide affords realistic strategies to prevent stress, relieve anxiety, and get rid of terrible questioning patterns whilst retaining a harmonious dwelling space.

The book begins by introducing the concept of "Time questioning" – a revolutionary technique that emphasises managing time and intellectual litter concurrently. As opposed to focusing totally on decluttering physical areas, Time questioning encourages readers to prioritise their intellectual well-being by way of dealing with their time successfully and fostering a nice attitude.

Readers learn how to discover sources of fear and tension in their houses and minds, gaining treasured insights into the relationship among their physical surroundings and intellectual fitness. via thought-upsetting sporting events and sensible hints, they discover a way to enforce strategies to manipulate and decrease anxiety levels, domesticate mindfulness practices, and vent bad minds and beliefs.

The writer gives actual-existence testimonies and examples of individuals who've transformed their houses and minds through the use of Time thinking standards, inspiring readers to embark on their personal journey in the direction of stability and peace. From prioritising responsibilities and keeping a muddle-free home to embracing mindfulness practices and fostering a positive attitude, this book offers a comprehensive roadmap for achieving intellectual clarity and a stress-free living surroundings.

Whether or not you're suffering with crush, anxiety, or terrible questioning styles, "Time assume: Manipulate your home without Decluttering Your mind" offers a holistic method to reclaim manipulation over your lifestyles. Through realistic advice, relatable anecdotes, and actionable techniques, readers will find out a way to create a domestic environment that nurtures well-being, fosters productivity, and promotes a feel of inner calm and fulfilment.

www.ingramcontent.com/pod-product-compliance
Lightning Source LLC
Chambersburg PA
CBHW050320230526
45471CB00005B/2273